AGAINST ALL ODDS

100 Motivational Quotes for Entrepreneurs to Push Beyond Challenges

LITERARY MUSE

FAQ'S ABOUT THIS BOOK

WHO IS THIS BOOK FOR?

This book is ideal for entrepreneurs, business professionals, managers, and anyone seeking inspiration in their careers. Whether you're starting out or looking to re-energize your path, the book offers valuable insights for various stages of professional growth.

WHAT IS THE PURPOSE OF THIS BOOK?

This book aims to empower and motivate readers with a curated collection of impactful business quotes from notable figures. Each quote is accompanied by an explanation that provides deeper insights into its meaning, encouraging readers to apply these principles to their professional lives and entrepreneurial journeys.

HOW ARE THE QUOTES SELECTED?

Quotes are chosen based on their relevance, motivational value, and practical application to business and personal growth. The selection spans a range of perspectives from successful business leaders, entrepreneurs, and influential thinkers to ensure that readers receive diverse, well-rounded inspiration.

HOW CAN I USE THIS BOOK EFFECTIVELY?

To get the most out of this book, read each quote and its accompanying explanation carefully, reflecting on how the message applies to your goals and challenges. You can use the quotes as daily affirmations, journal prompts, or share them with your team or network for added motivation. Many readers find it helpful to revisit specific quotes during pivotal moments for guidance and inspiration.

ARE THE QUOTES ORGANIZED IN ANY PARTICULAR WAY?

The quotes are presented in a way that allows each to stand alone with its explanation. There is no strict order, so you can browse and find quotes that resonate with you at any given moment, making it a versatile tool for continuous motivation.

HOW CAN I SHARE MY FEEDBACK ABOUT THE BOOK?

Feedback is highly valued! You can share your thoughts and suggestions through the publisher's website or by leaving a review on the platform where the book was purchased. Your insights are crucial in helping improve future editions and tailoring the content to meet readers' needs.

HOW CAN I SHARE MY FEEDBACK ABOUT THE BOOK?

Yes, the author plans to continue exploring motivational themes and may release additional volumes focusing on different sources or themes. Keep an eye out for announcements about new releases.

CAN I USE THIS BOOK TO SUPPORT TEAM OR COMPANY

Absolutely! Many readers find that these quotes spark valuable conversations, whether used in team meetings, leadership sessions, or company communications. The book can be a useful resource for encouraging team spirit, motivation, and professional growth.

QUOTE OUTLINE

INTRODUCTION

It was late autumn, and the leaves outside were falling in clusters, like burnt orange and gold coins cascading from the trees. As I sat by the window of my small home office, staring at a blank screen, I couldn't shake the feeling that I was, yet again, at a standstill. My business had started with so much promise, fueled by an idea I was passionate about, and the hope that I could create something impactful. Yet here I was, feeling the weight of doubt, watching the colorful leaves fall, feeling that same season of dormancy within myself.

When I began this journey, I had read countless books and articles, attended seminars, and watched hours of inspirational videos. I had heard the phrases a thousand times—*"Stay focused," "Don't give up," "You're one step away from success"*—but they had started to feel empty. The inspiration I'd once drawn from those words had faded, and I found myself wondering if I was just one more dreamer on the path to nowhere.

But then, as I let out a deep sigh, something occurred to me. Those words, those simple quotes that people often brushed off as cliché, were never meant to do the work for me. They were seeds, waiting to be planted in the fertile soil of my own belief, and it was up to me to water them, nurture them, and help them grow. They were sparks, and I needed to fan them into a flame.

It was then that I decided to write this book—a book of quotes, yes, but more than that, a collection of stepping stones designed to help anyone who's felt lost, discouraged, or weary in their journey. I wanted it to be a map, guiding readers back to the path they started on, reminding them of why they began, and reigniting the passion that first led them here. I wanted each quote to be more than just words on a page; I wanted each to come alive with meaning and

That quote taught me to stop focusing on short-term gains and start thinking about the bigger picture. I began to explore new ideas, to innovate, to take calculated risks. It reminded me that businesses thrive not just by following the rules but by daring to rewrite them.

SUCCESS AND ACHIEVEMENT

With time, my business began to grow. Clients came in, numbers rose, and I was able to see the fruits of my labor. But with success came a new set of challenges: staying grounded and remembering that the journey was far from over. A quote that kept me humble during this period was, *"It's fine to celebrate success, but it is more important to heed the lessons of failure."*

It reminded me that success isn't the end goal. It's a checkpoint on a longer journey. It reminded me that each milestone was simply a marker, and that there were still many more lessons to learn, more growth to achieve. It helped me see that success was not just about reaching the top; it was about how I got there and who I became along the way.

THE IMPORTANCE OF THIS BOOK

This book isn't just a collection of words; it's a companion for anyone on their own journey to success. It's for the dreamer who feels overwhelmed by the weight of ambition. It's for the entrepreneur who's doubting their ability to lead. It's for the go-getter who's facing obstacles and needs a reminder that setbacks are simply stepping stones.

Each quote within these pages is a piece of wisdom, a spark waiting to ignite the fire within you. As you read through this book, I hope you find something that speaks to you, something that gives you the strength to keep going, even when the path gets rocky. I hope you find the courage to push past your fears, the clarity to align your actions with your purpose, and the resilience to turn every failure into fuel.

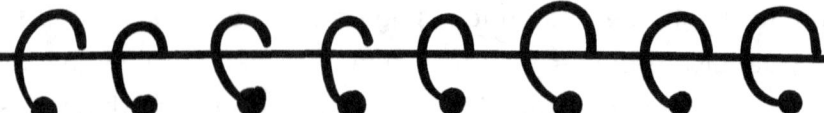

"Don't be distracted by criticism. Remember – the only taste of success some people get is to take a bite out of you."

ZIG ZIGLAR

EXPLANATION

Zig Ziglar was a renowned motivational speaker and author, known for his sales training and inspirational quotes.

His teachings emphasize the importance of a positive mindset and perseverance in the face of adversity. This quote serves as a reminder that criticism often stems from jealousy or insecurity. Instead of letting it deter you, focus on your goals and the value you provide. Successful entrepreneurs know how to filter constructive feedback from negativity, using it as fuel for their journey rather than a roadblock.

ACTION STEPS

Identify a recent criticism you've received and assess its validity.

_____

_____

_____

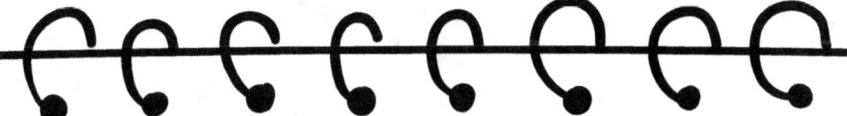

Revealing True Strength

"Only when the tide goes out do you discover who's been swimming naked."

WARREN BUFFETT

EXPLANATION

Warren Buffett is a legendary investor and the CEO of Berkshire Hathaway, widely regarded as one of the most successful investors of all time. This quote highlights the importance of transparency and preparedness in business. During prosperous times, weaknesses may be hidden, but challenges reveal true capabilities. Entrepreneurs must remain vigilant, ensuring they are building sustainable businesses that can withstand economic downturns.

ACTION STEPS

Evaluate your business's strengths and weaknesses regularly.

_____

_____

_____

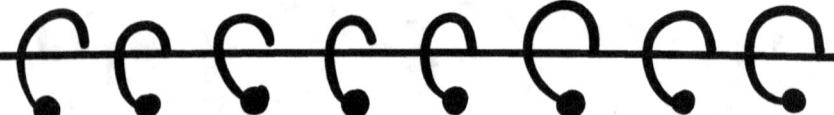

Finding Happiness in Success

"Success is not the key to happiness. Happiness is the key to success. If you love what you are doing, you will be successful."

ALBERT SCHWEITZER

EXPLANATION

Albert Schweitzer was a theologian, philosopher, and physician, famous for his humanitarian work and philosophy of life. His quote suggests that genuine passion is crucial for achieving success.

Entrepreneurs who derive joy from their work are more likely to be resilient, innovative, and ultimately successful. This highlights the importance of aligning personal values with professional pursuits to cultivate lasting fulfillment.

ACTION STEPS

Reflect on what truly makes you happy in your work.

_____

_____

_____

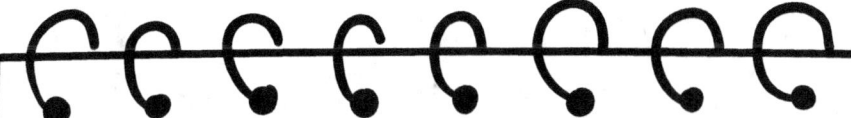

The Power of Ignorance

"Success is often achieved by those who don't know that failure is inevitable."

COCO CHANEL

EXPLANATION

Coco Chanel was a groundbreaking fashion designer who revolutionized women's fashion in the early 20th century.

This quote implies that an uninhibited mindset can lead to success. Often, the fear of failure holds many back, but those who embrace risk without the burden of this fear may achieve remarkable things. Entrepreneurs can benefit from adopting a bold approach, allowing themselves to innovate and explore new avenues without the paralyzing fear of failure.

ACTION STEPS

Take a bold step outside your comfort zone today.

_____

_____

_____

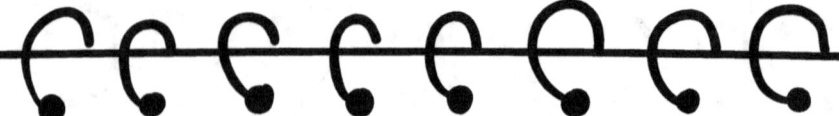

Turning Ideas into Reality

"It's not about ideas. It's about making ideas happen."

SCOTT BELSKY

EXPLANATION

Scott Belsky is a successful entrepreneur, author, and co-founder of Behance, a platform for creative professionals. His quote emphasizes the importance of execution over mere ideation. In the business world, having a great idea is just the beginning; the real challenge lies in turning that idea into a successful reality through diligent work and commitment. Entrepreneurs must focus on actionable steps that translate their vision into tangible outcomes.

ACTION STEPS

Create a detailed plan for an idea you have.

_____

_____

_____

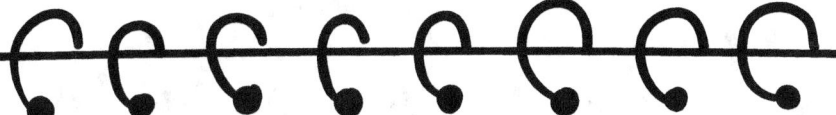

"Quality is more important than quantity. One home run is much better than two doubles."

STEVE JOBS

EXPLANATION

Steve Jobs, co-founder of Apple Inc., was known for his emphasis on innovation and quality. This quote illustrates that delivering exceptional quality in products or services can have a more significant impact than a larger quantity of mediocre offerings. In business, it's vital to focus on creating standout products that resonate with customers rather than spreading resources thin across many lesser projects.

ACTION STEPS

Assess the quality of your current offerings.

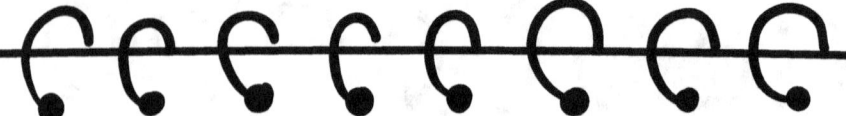

Work Comes Before Success

"The only place where success comes before work is in the dictionary."

VIDAL SASSOON

EXPLANATION

Vidal Sassoon was a renowned hairstylist and entrepreneur known for revolutionizing the hair industry. His quote serves as a reminder that hard work and dedication are prerequisites for success. Entrepreneurs should not expect success without putting in the necessary effort and commitment. This principle applies universally across all fields of business.

ACTION STEPS

Set a tangible goal and commit to working towards it.

_____

_____

_____

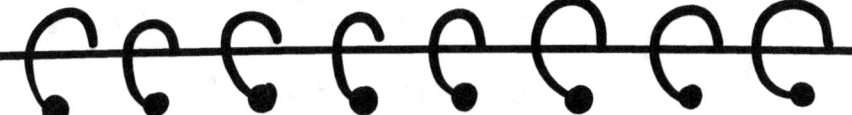

Fierce Strategy

"Play by the rules, but be ferocious."

PHIL KNIGHT

EXPLANATION

Phil Knight is the co-founder of Nike, a global leader in sportswear and athletic footwear. This quote underscores the importance of balancing integrity with a competitive spirit. In business, playing by the rules fosters trust and credibility, while ferocity in execution can help one stand out in a crowded market. Entrepreneurs must learn to be strategic and aggressive while adhering to ethical standards to thrive.

ACTION STEPS

Identify an area in your business where you can be more aggressive.

_____

_____

_____

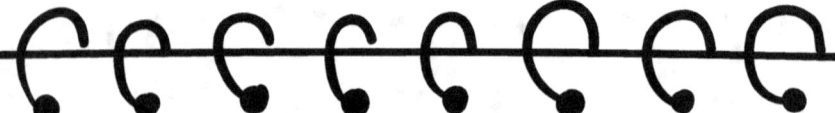

Framework for Success

"You don't have to be a genius or a visionary or even a college graduate to be successful. You just need a framework and a dream."

MICHAEL DELL

EXPLANATION

Michael Dell is the founder and CEO of Dell Technologies, known for revolutionizing the computer industry with direct-to-consumer sales. His quote reflects the belief that success is accessible to everyone with the right strategy and ambition. Entrepreneurs should focus on developing a clear framework for their goals, leveraging resources effectively, and cultivating their dreams into actionable plans.

ACTION STEPS

Draft a simple framework for your current business goals.

_____

_____

_____

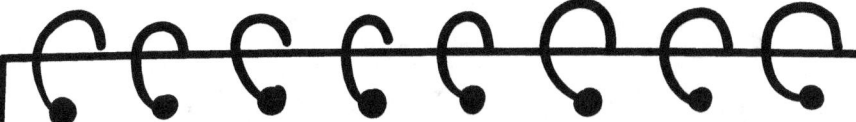

Driving Your Business

"If you don't drive your business, you will be driven out of business."

B.C. FORBES

EXPLANATION

B.C. Forbes was the founder of Forbes magazine and a prominent financial journalist. This quote emphasizes the importance of proactive leadership and engagement in business. Entrepreneurs must take charge of their operations, innovate, and adapt to market changes. A passive approach can lead to missed opportunities and eventual decline, making active participation crucial for success.

ACTION STEPS

Evaluate your current level of involvement in your business.

_____

_____

_____

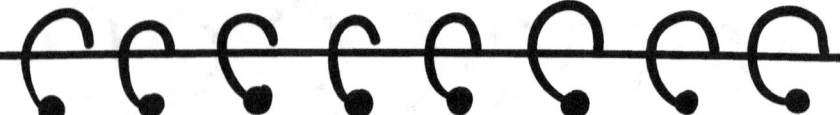

Embracing Failure

"Don't worry about failure; you only have to be right once."

DREW HOUSTON

EXPLANATION

Drew Houston is the co-founder and CEO of Dropbox, known for his entrepreneurial spirit and innovative approach to technology. His quote encourages a healthy perspective on failure. Rather than viewing it as a setback, entrepreneurs should see it as a stepping stone to eventual success. Embracing this mindset allows for experimentation and growth, where learning from failures can lead to breakthroughs.

ACTION STEPS

Identify a past failure and the lesson learned from it.

_____

_____

_____

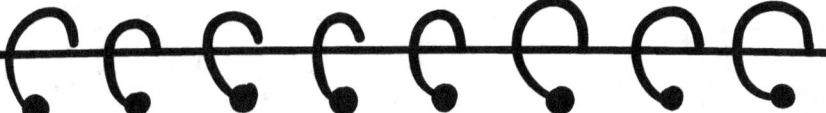

"The best way to learn is by doing. The only way to build a strong work ethic is getting your hands dirty."

ALEX SPANOS

EXPLANATION

Alex Spanos was a successful businessman and owner of the San Diego Chargers, known for his work ethic and entrepreneurial achievements. This quote emphasizes the value of practical experience in the learning process. Entrepreneurs should prioritize hands-on involvement in their ventures, as this fosters a deeper understanding of operations and cultivates a strong work ethic.

ACTION STEPS

Seek out a hands-on project related to your business.

_____

_____

_____

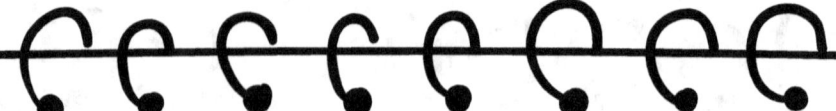

Passion Drives Success

"If you're passionate about something and you work hard, then I think you will be successful."

PIERRE OMIDYAR

EXPLANATION

Pierre Omidyar is the founder of eBay and a prominent entrepreneur and philanthropist. His quote highlights the intersection of passion and hard work as a formula for success. Entrepreneurs who are genuinely passionate about their ventures are more likely to persevere through challenges and achieve their goals. This underscores the importance of aligning personal interests with business endeavors for long-term fulfillment and achievement.

ACTION STEPS

Reflect on what you are passionate about in your work.

_____

_____

_____

Vision Over Money

"Chase the vision, not the money; the money will end up following you."

TONY HSIEH

EXPLANATION

Tony Hsieh was the CEO of Zappos, renowned for his unique approach to company culture and customer service. His quote emphasizes the importance of prioritizing a clear vision over immediate financial gains. Entrepreneurs should focus on building meaningful, customer-centric businesses that align with their core values, as financial success often follows when the vision is compelling.

ACTION STEPS

Clarify your business vision and goals.

_____

_____

_____

"You can't have everything you want, but you can have the things that really matter to you."

MARISSA MAYER

EXPLANATION

Marissa Mayer is a prominent tech executive and former CEO of Yahoo, known for her role at Google and her emphasis on user experience. Her quote underscores the importance of prioritization in life and business. Entrepreneurs must learn to focus on what truly matters, making strategic decisions that align with their values and long-term objectives. This approach fosters a sense of fulfillment and clarity in decision-making.

ACTION STEPS

Identify your top three priorities in your business.

_____

_____

_____

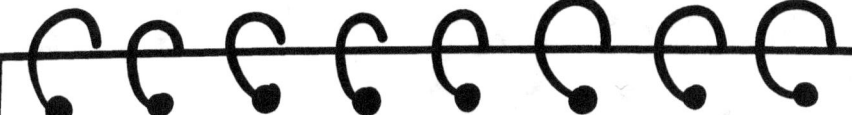

Action Over Words

"The way to get started is to quit talking and begin doing."

WALT DISNEY

EXPLANATION

Walt Disney was a visionary entrepreneur and the co-founder of The Walt Disney Company, known for his creativity and innovation in entertainment. His quote serves as a powerful reminder to take action rather than getting stuck in the planning phase. Entrepreneurs must adopt a bias for action, taking the necessary steps to bring their ideas to life instead of delaying progress through excessive discussion.

ACTION STEPS

Choose a small task related to your goals and complete it today.

_____

_____

_____

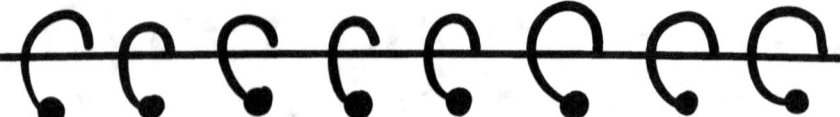

Good Over Original

"Don't try to be original, just try to be good."

PAUL RAND

EXPLANATION

Paul Rand was a celebrated graphic designer known for his influential work in corporate branding and design. This quote encourages entrepreneurs to focus on delivering quality rather than striving for originality. While innovation is valuable, the foundation of business success often lies in delivering good products and services that resonate with customers. Focusing on excellence can set one apart in competitive markets.

ACTION STEPS

Review your current offerings for areas of improvement.

_____

_____

_____

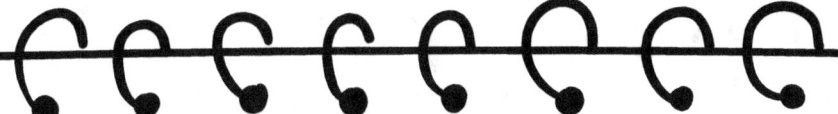
Learning from Failure

"Failure is simply the opportunity to begin again, this time more intelligently."

HENRY FORD

EXPLANATION

Henry Ford was a pioneering industrialist and founder of the Ford Motor Company, known for revolutionizing manufacturing through assembly line production. This quote reflects Ford's belief in learning from mistakes. Entrepreneurs should embrace failure as an essential part of the learning process, using insights gained to make better decisions in the future. This perspective fosters resilience and innovation.

ACTION STEPS

Analyze a recent failure for lessons learned.

_____

_____

_____

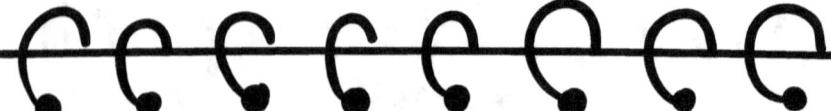

Bravery in Business

"Fortune always favors the brave, and never helps a man who does not help himself."

P.T. BARNUM

EXPLANATION

P.T. Barnum was an American showman and businessman, famous for founding the Ringling Bros. and Barnum & Bailey Circus. His quote emphasizes the importance of taking initiative and being bold in pursuit of success. Entrepreneurs must be willing to take calculated risks and actively seek opportunities, as fortune often rewards those who demonstrate courage and perseverance.

ACTION STEPS

Identify a risk you can take in your business this week.

_____

_____

_____

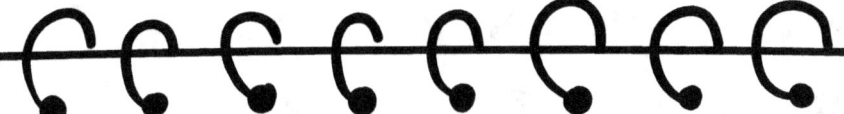

Pursuing Inspiration

"You can't wait for inspiration. You have to go after it with a club."

JACK LONDON

EXPLANATION

Jack London was an American author and journalist, known for his adventurous spirit and impactful storytelling. His quote serves as a call to action for entrepreneurs to proactively seek inspiration. Rather than waiting for creative ideas to strike, successful individuals take initiative to explore new avenues, experiences, and opportunities that spark innovation and growth.

ACTION STEPS

Set aside time this week to explore new ideas and inspirations.

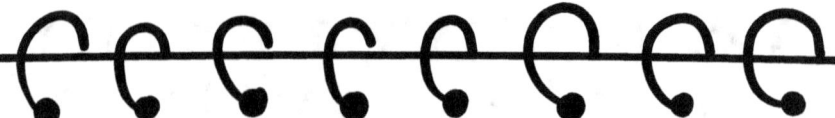

"Risk comes from not knowing what you're doing."

WARREN BUFFETT

EXPLANATION

Warren Buffett, often called the "Oracle of Omaha," is one of the most successful investors in history and the chairman and CEO of Berkshire Hathaway. His investment philosophy emphasizes the importance of understanding what you invest in and mitigating risks through knowledge.

This quote highlights that the unknown is the greatest source of risk in business. Successful entrepreneurs must educate themselves about their market, industry, and competitors to make informed decisions. Awareness and preparation can reduce uncertainty and lead to better outcomes.

ACTION STEPS

Assess a recent business decision and identify areas of uncertainty.

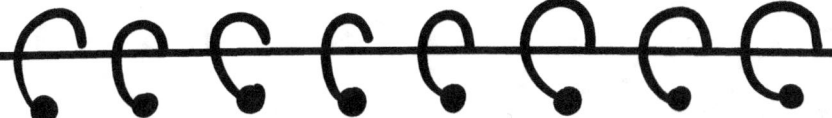

"An organization, no matter how well designed, is only as good as the people who live and work in it."

DEE HOCK

EXPLANATION

Dee Hock is the founder and former CEO of Visa Inc., a pioneer in electronic payments. His insights into organizational structure emphasize the significance of human capital. This quote conveys that the effectiveness of an organization is determined by the people who operate it, regardless of the frameworks in place. A well-designed organization without motivated and skilled individuals can falter. Investing in people, fostering collaboration, and nurturing a positive culture are vital for success.

ACTION STEPS

Evaluate your team's strengths and areas for growth.

_____

_____

_____

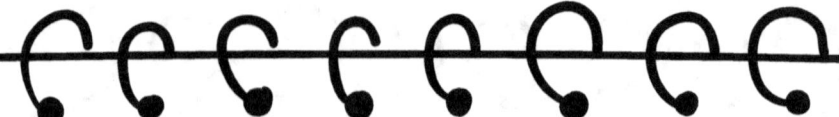
> ## "Never be limited by other people's limited imaginations."

MAE JEMISON

EXPLANATION

Mae Jemison is the first African American woman in space and a physician, engineer, and advocate for science education. Her accomplishments exemplify breaking barriers and challenging norms. This quote encourages entrepreneurs to think beyond conventional boundaries and embrace their unique visions. Often, the limitations imposed by others can stifle innovation. By believing in one's ideas and capabilities, entrepreneurs can pioneer new paths and achieve extraordinary results.

ACTION STEPS

List three unconventional ideas you have and explore them.

_____

_____

_____

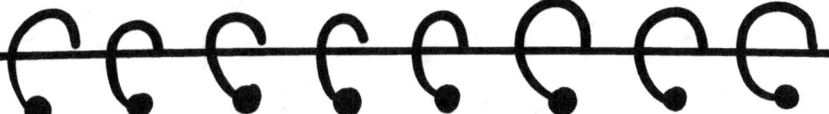

Opportunities Await

"Business opportunities are like buses; there's always another one coming."

RICHARD BRANSON

EXPLANATION

Richard Branson, the founder of the Virgin Group, is known for his adventurous spirit and diverse business ventures. This quote reflects Branson's optimistic view of entrepreneurship, suggesting that opportunities are abundant if you remain open to them. Just as buses continuously arrive, new ideas and chances arise constantly in business. Entrepreneurs must stay alert, adaptable, and willing to pivot when opportunities present themselves.

ACTION STEPS

Identify a recent opportunity you missed and analyze it.

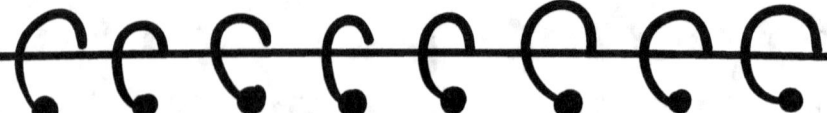

Learning from Failure

"It's fine to celebrate success, but it is more important to heed the lessons of failure."

BILL GATES

EXPLANATION

Bill Gates, co-founder of Microsoft, is one of the most influential figures in the tech industry and philanthropy. His quote stresses the value of learning from failures rather than merely celebrating successes. While achieving goals is essential, understanding the mistakes made along the way provides crucial insights for future endeavors. Embracing failure as a teacher can foster resilience and innovation, leading to greater long-term success.

ACTION STEPS

Reflect on a recent failure and identify key lessons learned.

_____

_____

_____

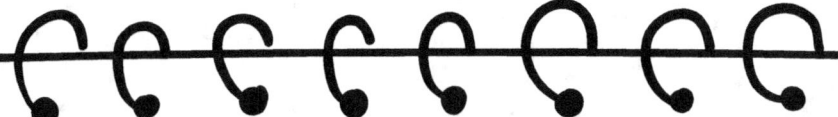

Work Hard, Recognize Opportunity

"Opportunities are usually disguised as hard work, so most people don't recognize them."

ANN LANDERS

EXPLANATION

Ann Landers was a prominent advice columnist known for her insightful responses to personal and social issues. Her quote highlights the common misconception that opportunities are easy to spot. In reality, most opportunities require significant effort and perseverance to uncover. Entrepreneurs often need to work diligently and consistently to reveal the chances for growth and success hidden within challenges. A strong work ethic and resilience are essential in recognizing and capitalizing on these opportunities.

ACTION STEPS

Identify a challenging task and tackle it head-on.

_____

_____

_____

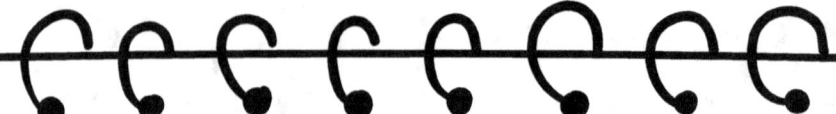

The Art of Change

"The secret of change is to focus all your energy not on fighting the old, but on building the new."

SOCRATES

EXPLANATION

Socrates, the ancient Greek philosopher, is known for his contributions to ethics and epistemology. This quote emphasizes the importance of proactive change rather than resisting it. In business, clinging to outdated practices can hinder progress. Instead of lamenting the past, entrepreneurs should invest their energy in innovating and creating new solutions. Embracing change and directing efforts toward future possibilities can lead to growth and success.

ACTION STEPS

Brainstorm new ideas for your business and prioritize them.

_____

_____

_____

"Success usually comes to those who are too busy to be looking for it."

HENRY DAVID THOREAU

EXPLANATION

Henry David Thoreau was an American essayist and philosopher known for his works on nature and individualism. This quote underscores the notion that success is often the byproduct of hard work and dedication rather than a direct pursuit. Entrepreneurs who focus on their tasks and responsibilities tend to create opportunities for success naturally. By remaining engrossed in meaningful work, one may find that success often follows.

ACTION STEPS

Dedicate time each day to focus on productive tasks.

_____

_____

_____

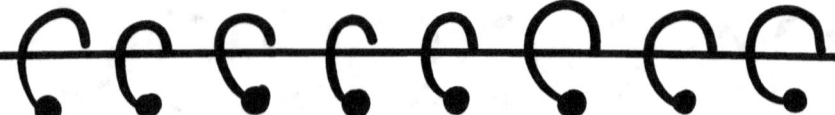

Heart and Business

"To be successful, you have to have your heart in your business, and your business in your heart."

THOMAS WATSON

EXPLANATION

Thomas Watson, the founder of IBM, transformed the company into a leader in the technology sector. His quote emphasizes the importance of passion in entrepreneurship. Success in business often stems from a genuine connection to one's work. When entrepreneurs invest their emotions and energy into their ventures, they create a more profound impact, fostering loyalty and resilience. This dedication can inspire teams and attract customers who resonate with the company's mission.

ACTION STEPS

Reflect on your passion and how it aligns with your business.

_____

_____

_____

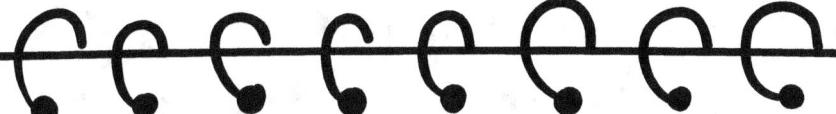

The Evolution of Brands

"Brands mature over time, like a marriage. The bond you feel with your spouse is different than when you first met each other."

GARY VAYNERCHUK

EXPLANATION

Gary Vaynerchuk is an entrepreneur and social media expert known for his work in digital marketing and e-commerce. This quote compares the evolution of brand relationships to those of marriage, highlighting that as brands grow, so too does the relationship with customers. Initially, brands may evoke excitement and novelty, but over time, they develop deeper connections based on trust and loyalty. Understanding this evolution can help businesses strategize their customer engagement efforts.

ACTION STEPS

Map out the stages of your brand's relationship with customers.

_____

_____

_____

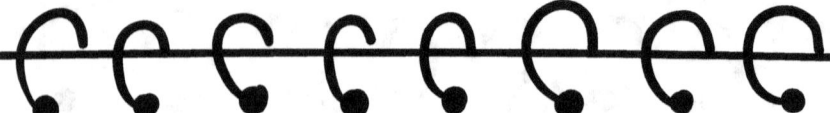

Simplicity in Success

"You only have to do a very few things right in your life so long as you don't do too many things wrong."

WARREN BUFFETT

EXPLANATION

Warren Buffett's wisdom emphasizes that success does not require perfection but rather a focus on making a few critical decisions correctly while avoiding significant mistakes. In the complex world of business, it's crucial to concentrate on a handful of impactful actions that lead to success. By prioritizing the essentials and minimizing errors, entrepreneurs can navigate their paths more effectively and achieve their goals.

ACTION STEPS

Identify key areas to focus on in your business strategy.

_____

_____

_____

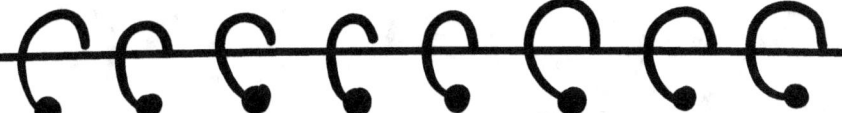

Luck and Preparation

"I feel that luck is preparation meeting opportunity."

OPRAH WINFREY

EXPLANATION

Oprah Winfrey, a media mogul and philanthropist, has built a legacy of influence and inspiration. Her quote suggests that what many perceive as luck often results from being well-prepared when opportunities arise. Successful entrepreneurs are proactive in developing their skills, knowledge, and resources, ensuring they are ready to seize chances when they present themselves. This mindset empowers individuals to create their luck through dedication and hard work.

ACTION STEPS

Prepare for potential opportunities by enhancing your skills.

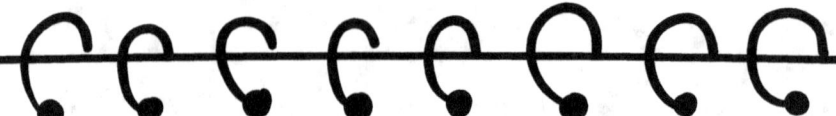

Legacy in Everyday Actions

"Please think about your legacy, because you're writing it every day."

GARY VAYNERCHUK

EXPLANATION

Gary Vaynerchuk emphasizes the importance of being mindful of the impact of daily actions on long-term legacy. As a digital entrepreneur and social media personality, he understands the weight of reputation in business. Every decision, interaction, and project contributes to the narrative one leaves behind. Entrepreneurs should be intentional about their choices, recognizing that their actions shape their legacy and influence their personal and professional lives.

ACTION STEPS

Write down what kind of legacy you want to leave behind.

_____

_____

_____

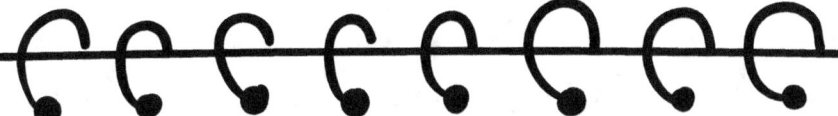

Taking Risks for Greatness

"If you are not willing to risk the usual, you will have to settle for the ordinary."

JIM ROHN

EXPLANATION

Jim Rohn was an influential motivational speaker and author, known for his impactful philosophies on personal development and entrepreneurship. This quote urges individuals to embrace risk and step outside their comfort zones. The path to greatness often requires venturing into the unknown and challenging the status quo. Entrepreneurs must be willing to take calculated risks to unlock their potential and achieve extraordinary results, rather than settling for mediocrity.

ACTION STEPS

Identify a risk you've been avoiding and take a step toward it.

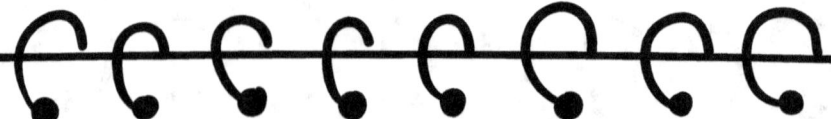

Customer Complaints as Opportunities

"Statistics suggest that when customers complain, business owners and managers ought to get excited about it."

ZIG ZIGLAR

EXPLANATION

Zig Ziglar was a renowned motivational speaker and author known for his work in sales and personal development. His quote emphasizes the value of customer feedback, particularly complaints. Rather than viewing complaints negatively, entrepreneurs should see them as opportunities for improvement and growth. Addressing concerns can enhance customer satisfaction and loyalty, leading to a stronger business model. Analyzing complaints can reveal insights into consumer needs and preferences.

ACTION STEPS

Review recent customer feedback and identify patterns.

_____

_____

_____

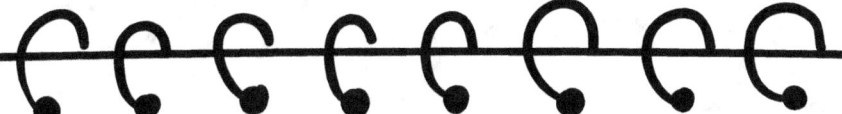

The Journey to Success

"If you really look closely, most overnight successes took a long time."

STEVE JOBS

EXPLANATION

Steve Jobs, co-founder of Apple Inc., is celebrated for his innovations and visionary leadership in technology. His quote reminds us that perceived overnight successes often result from years of hard work and perseverance. Behind every successful entrepreneur lies a story of dedication, learning, and overcoming challenges. This perspective encourages aspiring entrepreneurs to remain patient and committed, understanding that significant achievements often take time and effort to realize.

ACTION STEPS

Reflect on your journey and recognize the time invested in your goals.

_____

_____

_____

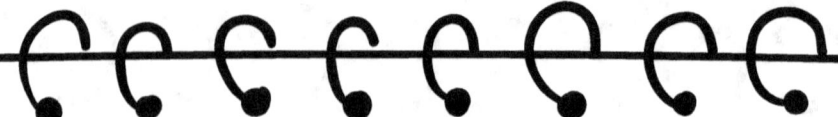

Dream Big

"Unless you dream, you're not going to achieve anything."

RICHARD BRANSON

EXPLANATION

Richard Branson's entrepreneurial spirit and adventurous lifestyle exemplify the importance of dreaming big. This quote emphasizes that dreams are the seeds of achievement. Entrepreneurs must envision their goals and aspirations to create tangible outcomes. Without dreams, individuals may lack the motivation to pursue ambitious projects or make significant changes. By cultivating a clear vision, entrepreneurs can inspire themselves and their teams to take bold actions toward achieving their objectives.

ACTION STEPS

Write down your biggest dreams and outline steps to achieve them.

_____

_____

_____

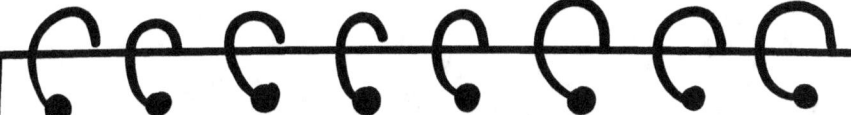

Pursuing Greatness

"Don't be afraid to give up the good to go for the great."

JOHN D. ROCKEFELLER

EXPLANATION

John D. Rockefeller was an American business magnate and philanthropist, known for his role in founding the Standard Oil Company. His quote encourages individuals to prioritize greatness over complacency. In business, settling for "good enough" can hinder progress and innovation. Entrepreneurs must be willing to make sacrifices and embrace change to reach their full potential. This mindset fosters an environment where striving for excellence becomes the norm, leading to remarkable achievements.

ACTION STEPS

Evaluate areas in your business where you might be settling.

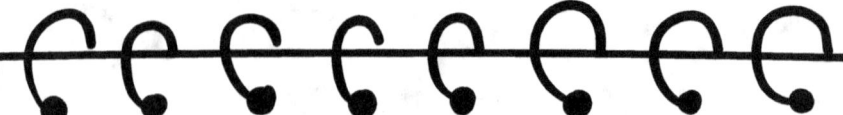

Dreams vs. Skills

"You must either modify your dreams or magnify your skills."

JIM ROHN

EXPLANATION

Jim Rohn emphasizes the balance between aspirations and the development of skills needed to achieve them. Entrepreneurs often face challenges in realizing their dreams; adapting those dreams to align with their abilities or enhancing their skills to meet their goals is essential. This quote highlights the importance of self-awareness and continuous learning in entrepreneurship. By acknowledging gaps and investing in skill enhancement, individuals can more effectively pursue their ambitions.

ACTION STEPS

Assess your skills and identify areas for improvement.

_____

_____

_____

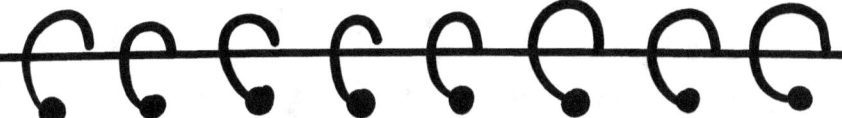

Persistence and Enthusiasm

"*Success is walking from failure to failure with no loss of enthusiasm.*"

WINSTON CHURCHILL

EXPLANATION

Winston Churchill, the British Prime Minister during WWII, is known for his leadership and resilience. This quote underscores the importance of persistence in the face of adversity. Success rarely comes without setbacks; maintaining enthusiasm and determination despite failures is crucial for entrepreneurs. This mindset fosters resilience and a positive attitude, enabling individuals to learn from mistakes and continue pursuing their goals.

ACTION STEPS

Reflect on past failures and how you responded to them.

_____

_____

_____

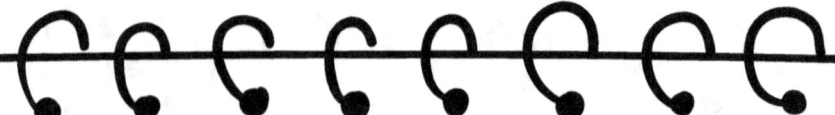

Embracing Mistakes as Growth

"In the real world, the smartest people are people who make mistakes and learn. In school, the smartest people don't make mistakes."

ROBERT KIYOSAKI

EXPLANATION

Robert Kiyosaki is an entrepreneur and author best known for his book "Rich Dad Poor Dad," which emphasizes financial education and investing. He highlights a critical distinction between formal education and real-world learning. In the business world, making mistakes can be invaluable for growth and innovation. Unlike traditional schooling, where errors may be stigmatized, the ability to learn from failures is what truly equips individuals for success. Kiyosaki advocates for a mindset that sees mistakes not as setbacks, but as stepping stones to greater knowledge and experience. This approach encourages entrepreneurs to take risks and embrace learning opportunities.

ACTION STEPS

Reflect on a recent mistake and identify lessons learned.

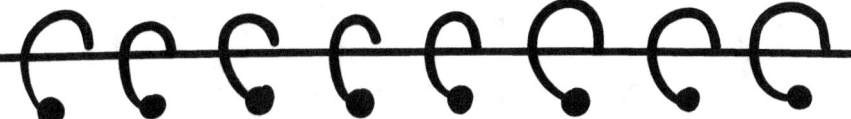

The Power of Presence

"Eighty percent of success is showing up."

WOODY ALLEN

EXPLANATION

Woody Allen is a celebrated filmmaker, actor, and comedian known for his unique storytelling style and prolific career in the entertainment industry. His quote underscores the fundamental truth that being present is crucial for achieving success. In the business realm, showing up can mean attending meetings, networking events, or simply putting in the effort to be engaged in your work. Many opportunities arise from being present and involved. Allen's statement serves as a reminder that commitment and consistency often outweigh talent or luck.

ACTION STEPS

Commit to being present in a specific aspect of your work.

_____

_____

_____

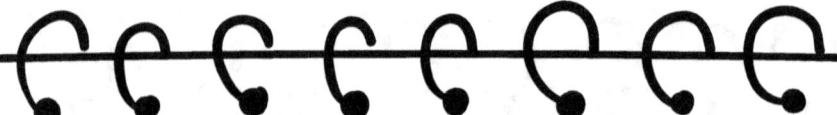

Action Over Words

"The way to get started is to quit talking and begin doing."

WALT DISNEY

EXPLANATION

Walt Disney was a pioneering figure in animation and entertainment, known for creating iconic characters and the Disneyland theme parks. This quote reflects his belief in the importance of action over discussion.

In entrepreneurship, it's easy to get caught up in planning and strategizing without taking the necessary steps to bring ideas to life. Disney encourages individuals to transition from the conceptual phase to the execution phase, emphasizing that progress comes from doing rather than just talking about plans. By acting decisively, entrepreneurs can turn their visions into reality.

ACTION STEPS

Identify one project you've been putting off and take action.

_____

_____

_____

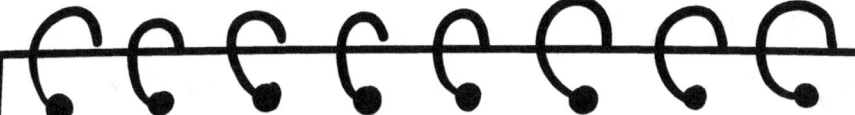

Beyond Monetary Motivation

"You reach a point where you don't work for money."

WALT DISNEY

EXPLANATION

Walt Disney, known for his creative genius and the establishment of the Disney brand, suggests that true fulfillment comes from passion rather than financial gain. In the business world, there often comes a time when success transcends monetary rewards, leading individuals to pursue their passions and contribute to something greater. Disney's insight encourages entrepreneurs to focus on what inspires them, suggesting that when work aligns with personal values and interests, the rewards extend beyond just financial success.

ACTION STEPS

Reflect on what drives your passion in your work.

_____

_____

_____

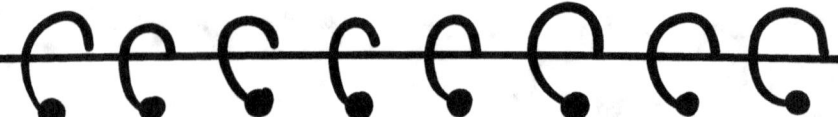

Failure as Redirection

"There is no such thing as failure. Failure is just life trying to move us in another direction."

OPRAH WINFREY

EXPLANATION

Oprah Winfrey, a media mogul and philanthropist, has built a legacy of empowerment and success through her influential work in television and publishing. Her perspective on failure reframes it as an opportunity for growth and redirection. In entrepreneurship, setbacks are often viewed negatively, but Winfrey's quote encourages a mindset shift: viewing failures as necessary steps toward success. This understanding fosters resilience and adaptability, allowing entrepreneurs to navigate challenges and emerge stronger.

ACTION STEPS

Identify a past failure and reframe it as a learning experience.

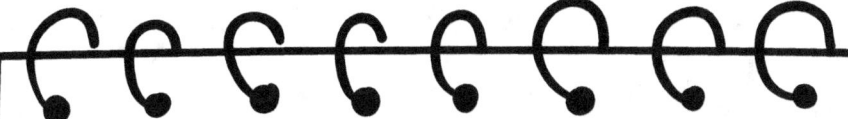

The Art of Leadership

"Leadership is the art of getting someone else to do something you want done because he wants to do it."

DWIGHT EISENHOWER

EXPLANATION

Dwight Eisenhower, the 34th President of the United States, was a military general and a key figure in World War II. His quote encapsulates the essence of effective leadership. In the business world, successful leaders inspire and motivate others to achieve shared goals, fostering a collaborative and driven team environment. Eisenhower's approach emphasizes the importance of understanding others' motivations and aligning them with organizational objectives. By cultivating this connection, leaders can create a more engaged and productive workforce.

ACTION STEPS

Reflect on your leadership style and its effectiveness.

_____

_____

_____

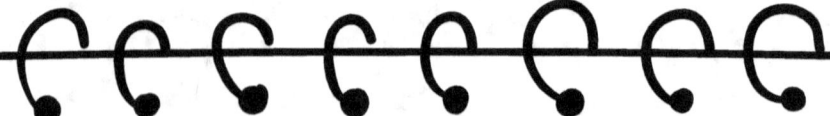

"If you don't like something, change it. If you can't change it, change your attitude. Don't complain."

MAYA ANGELOU

EXPLANATION

Maya Angelou was a renowned poet, memoirist, and civil rights activist whose words have inspired millions. Her quote advocates for proactive change and a positive mindset. In the business realm, challenges and obstacles are inevitable, but the ability to adapt and shift perspectives can determine success. Angelou emphasizes that instead of complaining about situations we can't control, we should either work towards change or adjust our mindset to find peace within our circumstances. This approach encourages resilience and innovation in the face of adversity.

ACTION STEPS

Identify an area of your life or business that needs change.

_____

_____

_____

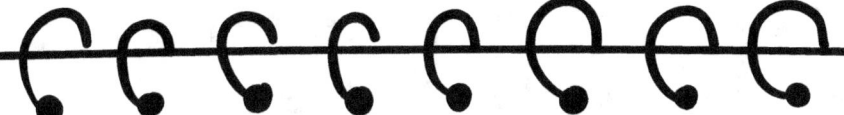

Your Work Defines You

"You are not your resume, you are your work."

SETH GODIN

EXPLANATION

Seth Godin is a prominent author and marketing expert known for his insights on the importance of storytelling and connection in business. His quote challenges the notion that a resume fully represents an individual's worth. In the entrepreneurial landscape, what truly defines us is not just our qualifications, but the impact of our work and contributions. Godin encourages entrepreneurs to focus on the value they bring to their endeavors and to view their work as a reflection of their identity and mission, fostering a deeper connection with their audience and clients.

ACTION STEPS

Evaluate how your work reflects your personal values and mission.

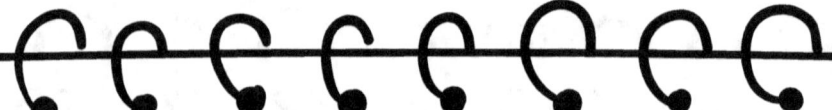

Building Your Own Legacy

"Build your own dreams, or someone else will hire you to build theirs."

FARRAH GRAY

EXPLANATION

Farrah Gray is a young entrepreneur and motivational speaker who achieved financial success at a young age. His quote emphasizes the importance of entrepreneurship and pursuing personal dreams. In a world where many work to fulfill others' visions, Gray encourages individuals to take control of their futures by building their own businesses and dreams. This mindset inspires creativity and ambition, driving individuals to carve out their own paths rather than settling for a life of working for someone else.

ACTION STEPS

Identify one dream you have and outline steps to pursue it.

_____

_____

_____

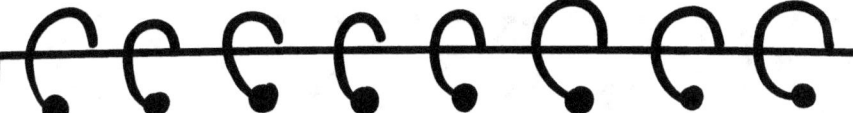

Seizing Opportunities

"The first one gets the oyster; the second gets the shell."

ANDREW CARNEGIE

EXPLANATION

Andrew Carnegie was a Scottish-American industrialist and philanthropist known for his role in the steel industry and his extensive philanthropic efforts. His quote highlights the importance of taking initiative and being the first to act on opportunities. In the competitive business world, prompt action can yield significant rewards, while hesitation may result in missed chances. Carnegie's perspective encourages entrepreneurs to be proactive and seize opportunities before they slip away, fostering a culture of decisiveness and courage in business.

ACTION STEPS

Reflect on a recent opportunity you missed and what you learned.

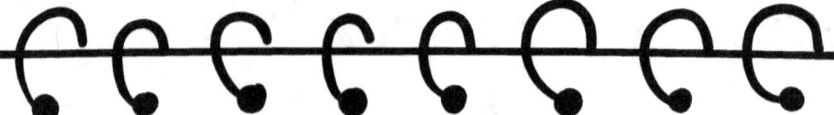

Living Boldly

"Live daringly, boldly, fearlessly. Taste the relish to be found in competition – in having put forth the best within you."

HENRY J. KAISER

EXPLANATION

Henry J. Kaiser was a prominent industrialist and shipbuilder known for his contributions during World War II and for founding Kaiser Permanente.

His quote embodies a spirit of boldness and competition, emphasizing the value of striving for excellence. In business, embracing competition and challenges can lead to personal growth and innovation. Kaiser's message encourages entrepreneurs to push their limits and embrace the thrill of competing, ultimately leading to greater achievements and self-discovery.

ACTION STEPS

Challenge yourself to step out of your comfort zone.

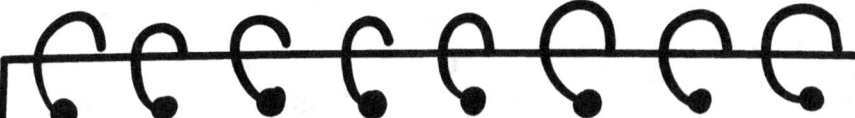

Claiming Your Power

"The most common way people give up their power is by thinking they don't have any."

ALICE WALKER

EXPLANATION

Alice Walker is an acclaimed author and activist, best known for her novel "The Color Purple." Her quote serves as a powerful reminder of the importance of recognizing and claiming one's personal power. In the business landscape, individuals often underestimate their influence and capabilities. Walker's perspective encourages entrepreneurs to acknowledge their strengths and assert themselves in their endeavors. By understanding and embracing their power, individuals can make impactful decisions and create meaningful change in their businesses and lives.

ACTION STEPS

Identify an area where you feel powerless and take action.

_____

_____

_____

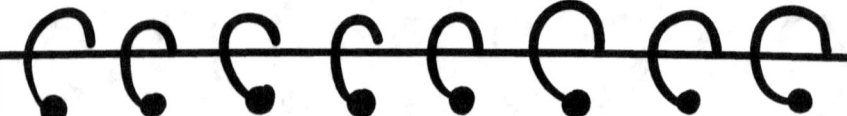

Avoiding the Bandwagon

"If you see a bandwagon, it's too late."

JAMES GOLDSMITH

EXPLANATION

James Goldsmith was a British businessman and environmentalist known for his keen insights on economics and business trends. His quote warns against the dangers of following trends rather than setting them. In the entrepreneurial world, waiting to jump on a bandwagon can lead to missed opportunities and competition. Goldsmith encourages innovators to forge their own paths and create unique offerings rather than simply following the crowd, fostering originality and leadership in business.

ACTION STEPS

Reflect on how you can create your own trends in your industry.

_____

_____

_____

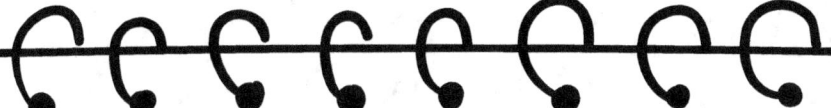

Courage to Pursue Dreams

"All our dreams can come true, if we have the courage to pursue them."

WALT DISNEY

EXPLANATION

Walt Disney's legacy as a visionary in entertainment is a testament to the power of dreams and creativity. This quote underscores the importance of courage in pursuing aspirations. In the world of entrepreneurship, many individuals harbor great ideas and dreams but fear taking the leap toward making them a reality. Disney's message encourages individuals to overcome their fears and take actionable steps toward their dreams, emphasizing that belief in oneself is the first step toward success.

ACTION STEPS

Write down one dream you want to pursue and outline steps to achieve it.

_____

_____

_____

"A man should never neglect his family for business."

WALT DISNEY

EXPLANATION

Walt Disney was not only a pioneer in animation but also a devoted family man. His quote highlights the significance of maintaining a balance between professional aspirations and personal relationships. In the fast-paced business world, it's easy to become consumed by work and neglect important connections at home. Disney's wisdom serves as a reminder that true success encompasses family, love, and relationships. By prioritizing family alongside business endeavors, individuals can lead more fulfilling and well-rounded lives.

ACTION STEPS

Reflect on your work-life balance and areas for improvement.

_____

_____

_____

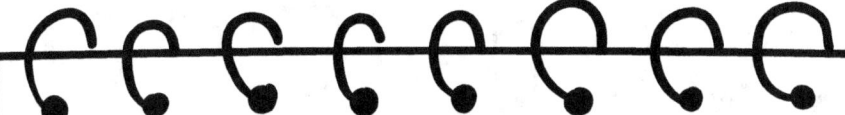

Living in the Present

"Look well to this day. Yesterday is but a dream and tomorrow is only a vision. But today well-lived makes every yesterday a dream of happiness and every tomorrow a vision of hope."

FRANCIS GRAY

EXPLANATION

Francis Gray, a poet and philosopher, emphasizes the importance of living in the present. His quote serves as a reminder that while it's essential to learn from the past and plan for the future, true fulfillment comes from how we engage with the present moment. In the context of entrepreneurship, focusing on today's tasks and opportunities can lead to greater productivity and satisfaction. By living fully in the present, individuals can create a foundation for future success and happiness.

ACTION STEPS

Practice mindfulness in your daily activities.

_____

_____

_____

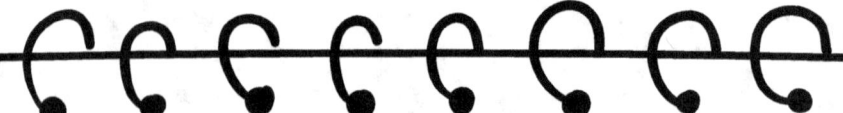

The Luck of Hard Work

"I find that the harder I work, the more luck I seem to have."

THOMAS JEFFERSON

EXPLANATION

Thomas Jefferson, the third President of the United States and a Founding Father, valued hard work and diligence. His quote encapsulates the relationship between effort and perceived luck. In the business world, success often results from consistent effort and perseverance. Jefferson's perspective challenges the notion that luck is purely random, suggesting that hard work creates opportunities for success and increases the chances of favorable outcomes. By dedicating themselves to their goals, entrepreneurs can position themselves to "get lucky."

ACTION STEPS

Commit to working hard on a specific goal for a set time.

_____

_____

_____

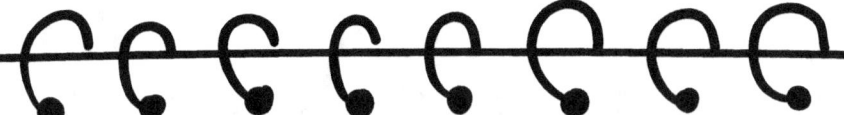

Winning as a Habit

"Winning is not a sometime thing; it's an all-time thing. You don't win once in a while, you don't do things right once in a while, you do them right all the time. Winning is habit. Unfortunately, so is losing."

VINCE LOMBARDI

EXPLANATION

Vince Lombardi, a legendary football coach, is renowned for his commitment to excellence and winning. His quote emphasizes that success is a continuous effort rather than an occasional occurrence. In the entrepreneurial landscape, establishing habits that promote success can lead to consistent achievements. Lombardi's perspective encourages individuals to develop a winning mindset, fostering discipline and dedication in their business practices, which ultimately leads to sustained success over time.

ACTION STEPS

Identify one habit that contributes to your success.

_____

_____

_____

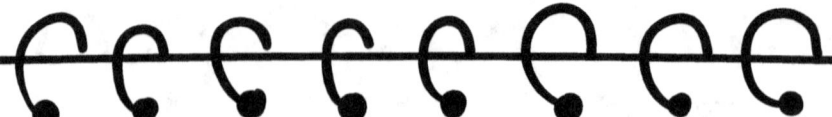

"Opportunities don't happen. You create them."

CHRIS GROSSER

EXPLANATION

Chris Grosser is an entrepreneur and author who emphasizes the proactive approach to opportunity creation. His quote highlights that waiting for opportunities to come is often futile; instead, individuals must take initiative and actively create their own chances for success. In the business world, this means identifying gaps in the market, networking, and being innovative. Grosser's message encourages entrepreneurs to be resourceful and to cultivate an entrepreneurial mindset that seeks out possibilities rather than waiting passively.

ACTION STEPS

Brainstorm ways you can create opportunities in your field.

_____

_____

_____

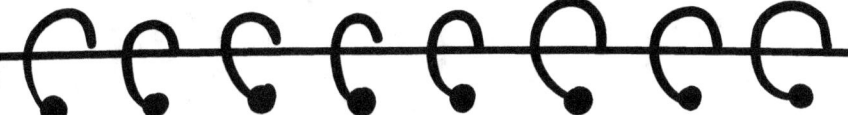

Desires Over Needs

"People rarely buy what they need. They buy what they want."

SETH GODIN

EXPLANATION

Seth Godin, a thought leader in marketing, stresses the significance of understanding consumer behavior. His quote reveals that emotions and desires often drive purchasing decisions more than practical needs. In the business realm, successful entrepreneurs must tap into the wants of their customers to create compelling products and services. Godin's insight encourages businesses to focus on building strong connections with their audience, identifying their desires, and crafting offerings that resonate deeply, leading to greater sales and loyalty.

ACTION STEPS

Research your target audience's desires and preferences.

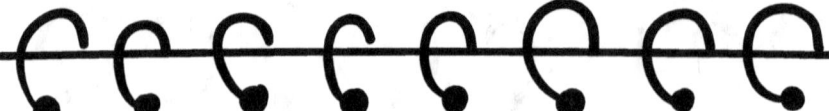

Fresh Perspectives

"To think creatively, we must be able to look afresh at what we normally take for granted."

GEORGE KNELLER

EXPLANATION

George Kneller was an influential educator and psychologist known for his contributions to the field of creativity and the arts. He emphasized the importance of viewing ordinary concepts with a new lens. In business, this approach encourages entrepreneurs to innovate and seek out hidden opportunities by challenging assumptions. By questioning the status quo, businesses can discover unique solutions and foster an environment of creativity that leads to success. The key is to embrace curiosity and openness to new ideas.

ACTION STEPS

Identify an area in your business where you can apply fresh thinking.

_____

_____

_____

Finding Your Drive

"To succeed, you need to find something to hold on to, something to motivate you, something to inspire you."

TONY DORSETT

EXPLANATION

Tony Dorsett is a former professional American football player who was inducted into the Pro Football Hall of Fame. His dedication to sport and perseverance through challenges underscore the necessity of having a strong motivational foundation in any pursuit, especially in business. In the entrepreneurial world, maintaining inspiration and motivation is crucial for overcoming obstacles and achieving long-term goals. Dorsett's insight reminds us to identify our core passions and values to drive our endeavors forward.

ACTION STEPS

Write down your top three motivators and revisit them regularly.

_____

_____

_____

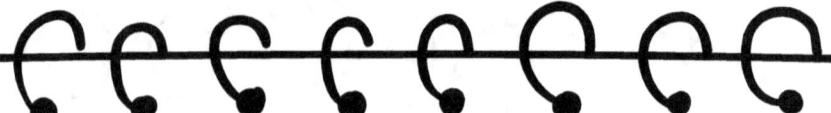

Pioneering Mindset

"If you're competitor-focused, you have to wait until there is a competitor doing something. Being customer-focused allows you to be more pioneering."

JEFF BEZOS

EXPLANATION

Jeff Bezos, the founder of Amazon, revolutionized e-commerce and retail through a relentless focus on customer needs rather than merely competing with others. His insights highlight the importance of anticipating customer demands and innovating accordingly. By prioritizing the customer experience, businesses can create unique offerings and set themselves apart from the competition. Bezos's philosophy encourages entrepreneurs to listen actively to their customers and adapt to their evolving needs.

ACTION STEPS

Conduct a survey to gather customer feedback on your product or service.

_____

_____

_____

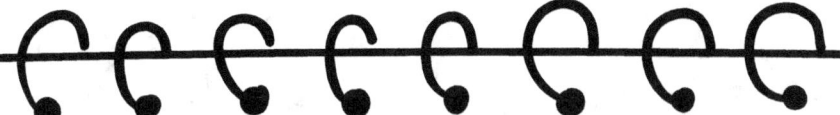

Executing Ideas

"There's no shortage of remarkable ideas; what's missing is the will to execute them."

SETH GODIN

EXPLANATION

Seth Godin is a renowned author and marketing expert known for his thoughts on creativity and leadership. He stresses that while ideas are abundant, the true challenge lies in executing them effectively. In business, many great concepts remain unrealized due to a lack of action and commitment. Godin's quote serves as a powerful reminder for entrepreneurs to not only generate ideas but also take actionable steps to turn those ideas into reality, emphasizing that execution is the key to success.

ACTION STEPS

Create an action plan for one of your great ideas that you've been postponing.

_____

_____

_____

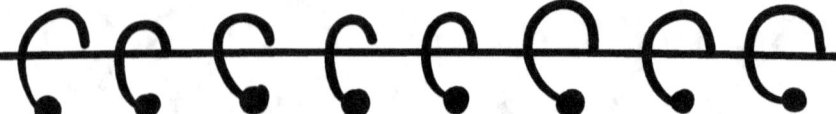

Embracing Change

"Change is not a threat; it's an opportunity. Survival is not the goal; transformative success is."

SETH GODIN

EXPLANATION

Again, Seth Godin offers profound insights, this time on the nature of change. He is a leading voice in marketing and business strategy, advocating for viewing change as a catalyst for growth rather than a setback. Embracing change allows businesses to adapt, innovate, and find new paths to success. Godin's perspective encourages entrepreneurs to seek opportunities in every challenge, positioning themselves not just to survive but to thrive in an ever-evolving marketplace.

ACTION STEPS

Identify a recent change in your industry and brainstorm how you can adapt positively.

_____

_____

_____

"Yesterday's home runs don't win today's games."

BABE RUTH

EXPLANATION

Babe Ruth, one of the most iconic figures in baseball history, epitomized excellence and innovation in sports. His quote emphasizes the necessity of staying relevant and continuously improving rather than resting on past successes. For entrepreneurs, this translates to the need for constant evolution and adaptation in their strategies and offerings. Ruth's wisdom reminds business leaders that staying ahead of the curve is essential for long-term success and growth.

ACTION STEPS

Assess how your current strategies align with today's market needs.

_____

_____

_____

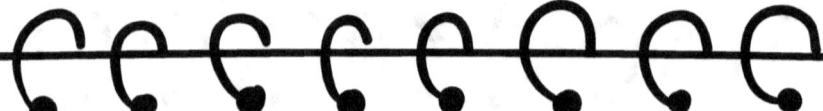
Quality over Cost

"There is one rule for the industrialist and that is: make the best quality goods possible at the lowest cost possible, paying the highest wages possible."

HENRY FORD

EXPLANATION

Henry Ford was a pioneering industrialist who revolutionized manufacturing with his introduction of assembly line production. His commitment to quality, cost efficiency, and fair labor practices set standards in the industry. Ford's philosophy underscores the importance of balancing quality with cost-effectiveness in business. By focusing on high-quality goods and fair compensation for workers, businesses can foster loyalty and achieve long-term sustainability in the marketplace.

ACTION STEPS

Evaluate your current production methods to enhance quality without raising costs.

_____

_____

_____

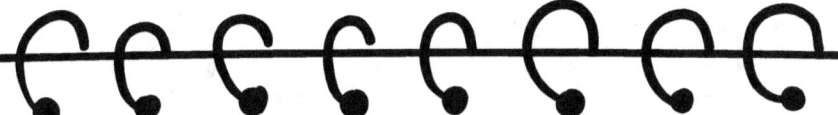

Innovation and Criticism

"If you never want to be criticized, for goodness' sake don't do anything new."

JEFF BEZOS

EXPLANATION

Jeff Bezos, again shedding light on innovation, emphasizes the inherent risk of criticism that comes with trying new things. As the founder of Amazon, he is well-acquainted with both the accolades and critiques of innovation. His quote serves as a reminder that criticism is a natural part of the entrepreneurial journey, particularly when venturing into uncharted territory. Entrepreneurs should embrace this reality and view criticism as a stepping stone toward improvement and growth rather than a deterrent.

ACTION STEPS

Prepare a strategy to handle criticism constructively when pursuing new ideas.

_____

_____

_____

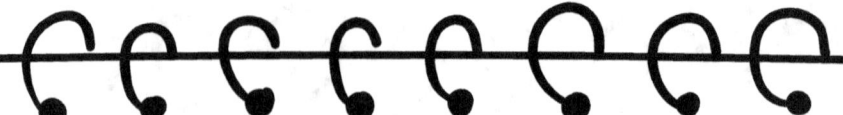

Strategic Patience

"Never interrupt your enemy when he is making a mistake."

NAPOLEON BONAPARTE

EXPLANATION

Napoleon Bonaparte, a brilliant military strategist and leader, understood the importance of patience in achieving victory. His quote emphasizes the value of allowing competitors to make mistakes rather than rushing to intervene. In business, this strategy can be crucial; understanding when to act and when to observe can provide a significant advantage. Entrepreneurs can learn to be patient and strategic, capitalizing on their competitors' missteps while focusing on their own goals.

ACTION STEPS

Analyze your competitors' actions to identify potential opportunities.

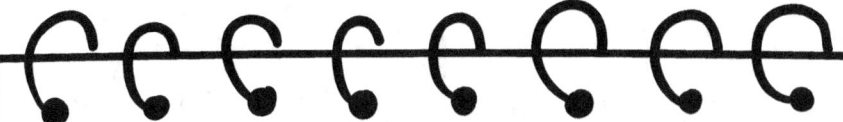

Giving Value

"The man who will use his skill and constructive imagination to see how much he can give for a dollar, instead of how little he can give for a dollar, is bound to succeed."

HENRY FORD

EXPLANATION

Henry Ford's quote reflects his commitment to value creation in business. By emphasizing the importance of giving more than what is expected, Ford established a framework for building strong customer relationships and loyalty. His approach highlights that businesses that focus on adding value rather than minimizing costs are more likely to achieve sustainable success. Ford's vision encourages entrepreneurs to think creatively about how to enhance their offerings and customer experiences.

ACTION STEPS

Develop a strategy to increase the value of your offerings without raising prices.

_____

_____

_____

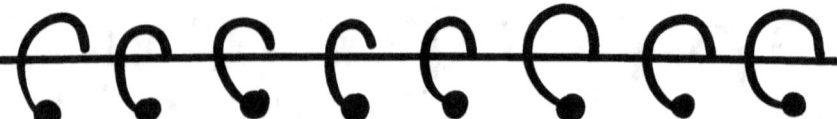

Learning from Discontent

"Your most unhappy customers are your greatest source of learning."

BILL GATES

EXPLANATION

Bill Gates, co-founder of Microsoft, is one of the most influential figures in technology and business. His quote reflects the critical importance of customer feedback, particularly negative feedback. Gates suggests that unhappy customers can provide valuable insights into areas for improvement. For entrepreneurs, actively seeking and analyzing this feedback can lead to significant growth and enhancement of products and services, ultimately fostering customer loyalty and satisfaction.

ACTION STEPS

Create a system for regularly gathering and analyzing customer feedback.

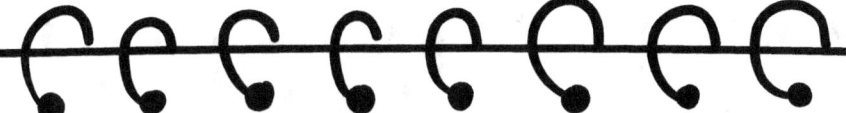

"It is better to fail in originality than to succeed in imitation."

HERMAN MELVILLE

EXPLANATION

Herman Melville, an American novelist and poet, is best known for his work "Moby-Dick." His quote encourages individuals to embrace originality and creativity rather than merely replicating the success of others. In the business landscape, originality is essential for differentiation and innovation. Melville's perspective reminds entrepreneurs that while the fear of failure can be daunting, the pursuit of unique ideas and approaches is where true potential lies, leading to breakthrough innovations.

ACTION STEPS

Brainstorm a list of unique ideas that set your business apart from competitors.

_____

_____

_____

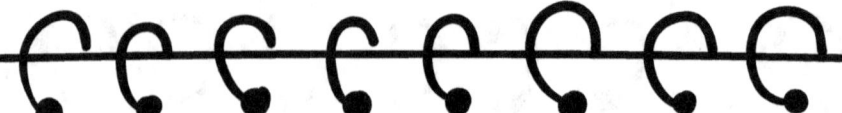

"Beware of any enterprise requiring new clothes."

HENRY DAVID THOREAU

EXPLANATION

Henry David Thoreau, an American philosopher and writer, is known for his advocacy of simplicity and minimalism. His quote suggests caution regarding ventures that demand significant investment or adornment, implying that the essence of business should not rely on superficial aspects. In the entrepreneurial realm, this insight emphasizes the importance of focusing on core values and authentic offerings rather than getting caught up in trends or appearances. Thoreau's wisdom encourages entrepreneurs to assess the true value of their endeavors.

ACTION STEPS

Reflect on your business practices and eliminate unnecessary complexities.

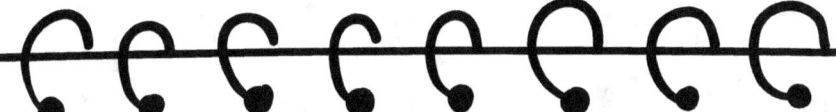

Confronting Fear

"We generate fears while we sit. We overcome them by action. Fear is nature's way of warning us to get busy."

DR. HENRY LINK

EXPLANATION

Dr. Henry Link was a prominent psychologist known for his insights into human behavior and motivation. His quote addresses the universal experience of fear and highlights the necessity of taking action to overcome it. For entrepreneurs, fear can often be paralyzing, preventing them from pursuing new opportunities. Link's perspective encourages business leaders to confront their fears directly through proactive measures, transforming anxiety into motivation for growth and exploration.

ACTION STEPS

Take one small action today that pushes you outside your comfort zone.

_____

_____

_____

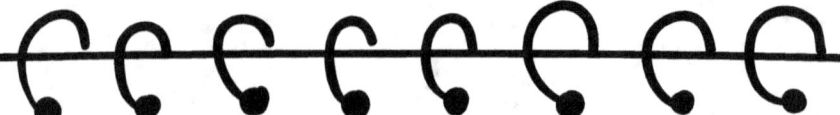

Rethinking Productivity

"Early to bed and early to rise probably indicates unskilled labor."

JOHN CIARDI

EXPLANATION

John Ciardi was an American poet and translator known for his wit and keen observations about society. His quote challenges the traditional notion of productivity, suggesting that hard work does not always correlate with skill or effectiveness. For entrepreneurs, this insight prompts a reevaluation of how they define productivity and success. It encourages a focus on working smart rather than simply putting in long hours, highlighting the importance of strategy, creativity, and efficiency in achieving goals.

ACTION STEPS

Reflect on your daily routines and identify areas for increased efficiency.

_____

_____

_____

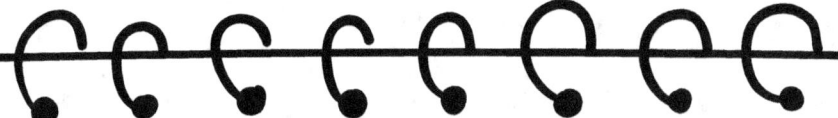

"Never put off until tomorrow what you can avoid altogether."

UNKNOWN

EXPLANATION

This anonymous quote highlights the importance of decisiveness and timely action in business. While the origin is unknown, the sentiment resonates deeply with entrepreneurs who often grapple with procrastination and inaction. In the fast-paced business world, delaying decisions can lead to missed opportunities and stagnation. The message here is clear: avoid unnecessary delays and make proactive choices to keep momentum going.

ACTION STEPS

Create a list of tasks you've been postponing and prioritize them for completion.

_____

_____

_____

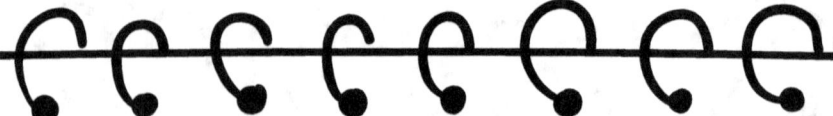

Fun in Business

"A business has to be involving, it has to be fun, and it has to exercise your creative instincts."

RICHARD BRANSON

EXPLANATION

Richard Branson, the founder of the Virgin Group, is renowned for his adventurous spirit and innovative approach to business. His quote encapsulates the belief that business should not only be about profit but also about enjoyment and creativity. Branson's philosophy encourages entrepreneurs to cultivate a work environment that fosters engagement and creativity, leading to more innovative ideas and a more motivated team. This approach can also enhance customer experiences and brand loyalty.

ACTION STEPS

Assess your work culture and find ways to make it more enjoyable and engaging.

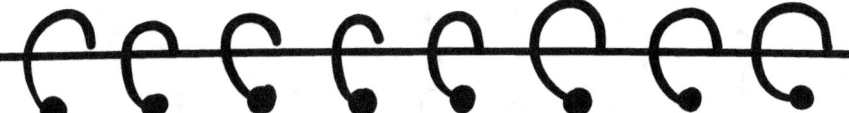

"Success is a lousy teacher. It seduces smart people into thinking they can't lose."

BILL GATES

EXPLANATION

Bill Gates offers a powerful perspective on the nature of success and failure. His experience as a tech entrepreneur illustrates that success can breed complacency, making individuals overlook the lessons that failure can teach. Gates emphasizes the importance of maintaining humility and a learning mindset, even amidst success. For entrepreneurs, recognizing that every setback provides valuable insights is crucial for continuous improvement and resilience in the face of challenges.

ACTION STEPS

Analyze a recent failure and identify key lessons learned from the experience.

_____

_____

_____

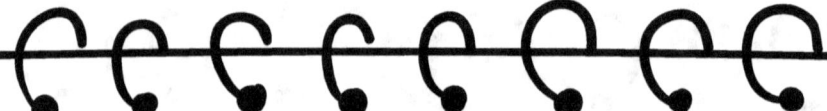

"Success is not final; failure is not fatal: It is the courage to continue that counts."

WINSTON S. CHURCHILL

EXPLANATION

Winston S. Churchill, the British Prime Minister during World War II, is celebrated for his leadership and resilience during times of crisis. His quote speaks to the transient nature of success and failure, highlighting that the true measure of a person is their perseverance in the face of challenges. For entrepreneurs, this mindset fosters resilience and determination, reminding them that the journey is ongoing and that courage is essential for navigating the ups and downs of business.

ACTION STEPS

Commit to a project or goal that you have been hesitant to pursue.

_____

_____

_____

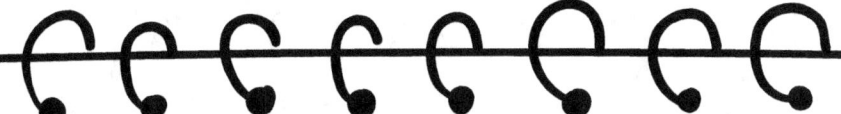

Product Quality First

"If you keep your eye on the profit, you're going to skimp on the product. But if you focus on making really great products, then the profits will follow."

STEVE JOBS

EXPLANATION

Steve Jobs, co-founder of Apple Inc., is known for his innovative vision and commitment to excellence in product design. His quote reflects the principle that prioritizing quality over immediate financial gain ultimately leads to greater success. By focusing on creating exceptional products, businesses can foster customer loyalty and long-term profitability. Jobs' philosophy encourages entrepreneurs to invest in their products and maintain a vision that transcends short-term financial objectives.

ACTION STEPS

Evaluate your product offerings and find ways to enhance quality and customer satisfaction.

_____

_____

_____

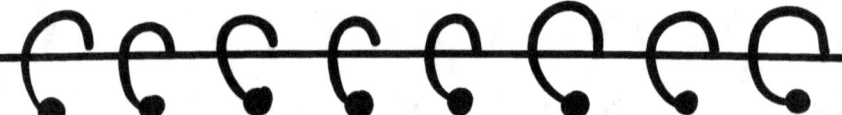

Pursuing Potential

"It is never too late to be what you might have been."

GEORGE ELIOT

EXPLANATION

George Eliot, a pen name for Mary Ann Evans, was a renowned English novelist and essayist known for her pioneering works in literature. She challenged societal norms through her writing, advocating for women's rights and personal agency. Her quote emphasizes the idea that individuals can always pursue their dreams and aspirations, regardless of age or circumstance. In the business world, this sentiment resonates with entrepreneurs who may feel limited by time or previous failures. It serves as a reminder that reinvention is always possible and that taking bold steps can lead to fulfilling one's true potential.

ACTION STEPS

Identify one dream or goal you've postponed and take the first step towards it.

_____

_____

_____

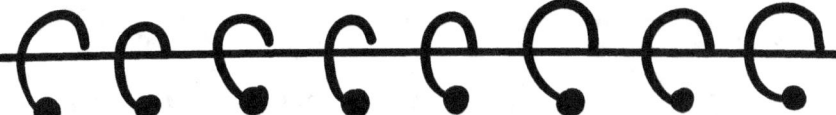

The Dream Makers

"You can design and create, and build the most wonderful place in the world. But it takes people to make the dream a reality."

WALT DISNEY

EXPLANATION

Walt Disney, an iconic figure in the entertainment industry, revolutionized animation and theme parks, creating a legacy of imagination and innovation. His quote highlights the importance of collaboration and teamwork in realizing visions. Disney's success was not solely due to his creativity but also the dedication and talent of the people he surrounded himself with. For entrepreneurs, this serves as a powerful reminder that while individual vision is important, success relies on the collective effort of a committed team to turn dreams into tangible results.

ACTION STEPS

Reflect on your current team dynamics and find ways to enhance collaboration.

_____

_____

_____

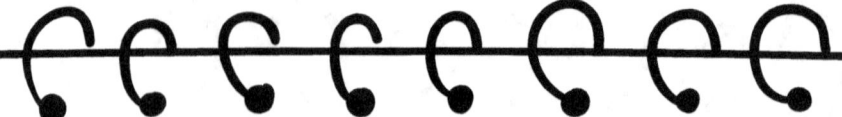

Transforming Wealth

"The moment you make passive income and portfolio income a part of your life, your life will change. Those words will become flesh."

ROBERT KIYOSAKI

EXPLANATION

Robert Kiyosaki is a successful entrepreneur, investor, and author of the best-selling book "Rich Dad Poor Dad." His teachings emphasize financial literacy and the importance of creating passive income streams. Kiyosaki's quote highlights how integrating various income sources can lead to financial freedom and transformative changes in one's lifestyle. Entrepreneurs can benefit from understanding that diversifying income through investments and business ventures can empower them to take control of their financial future and enhance their quality of life.

ACTION STEPS

Research different forms of passive income and create an action plan to implement one.

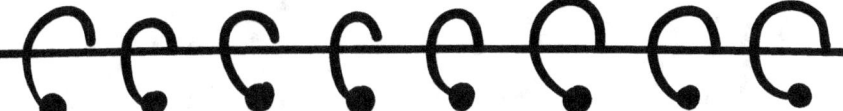
Value of Meaningful Work

"Far and away the best prize that life offers is the chance to work hard at work worth doing."

THEODORE ROOSEVELT

EXPLANATION

Theodore Roosevelt, the 26th President of the United States, was known for his dynamic personality and commitment to social reform. His quote reflects his belief in the importance of engaging in meaningful work that contributes positively to society. Roosevelt's life was a testament to the value of hard work, perseverance, and the pursuit of noble causes. For entrepreneurs, this quote serves as a reminder to focus not only on profitability but also on the impact and significance of their work in the world.

ACTION STEPS

Evaluate your current projects and identify which align with your core values.

_____

_____

_____

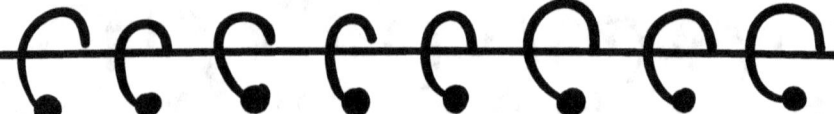

Strength in Emphasis

"The trick is in what one emphasizes. We either make ourselves miserable or we make ourselves strong. The amount of work is the same."

CARLOS CASTANEDA

EXPLANATION

Carlos Castaneda was an American author and anthropologist known for his writings on shamanism and spirituality. His quote explores the concept of perspective and the power of choice in shaping our experiences. Castaneda's work emphasizes that while challenges are inevitable, how we frame and respond to them can determine our strength and resilience. For entrepreneurs, this insight encourages a focus on positive thinking and a proactive approach to overcoming obstacles, transforming hardships into opportunities for growth.

ACTION STEPS

Reflect on a current challenge and reframe it in a positive light.

_____

_____

_____

Mindset of Winners

"The winners in life think constantly in terms of 'I can, I will, and I am.' Losers, on the other hand, concentrate on what they should have or would have done or what they can't do."

DENNIS WAITLEY

EXPLANATION

Dennis Waitley is a renowned motivational speaker and author known for his work on self-improvement and performance enhancement. His quote emphasizes the importance of a positive mindset in achieving success. Waitley's philosophy encourages individuals to adopt an empowering narrative that focuses on possibilities rather than limitations. For entrepreneurs, cultivating a mindset that prioritizes action and possibility can lead to greater achievements and a more resilient approach to challenges.

ACTION STEPS

Create a personal mantra that emphasizes your strengths and capabilities.

_____

_____

_____

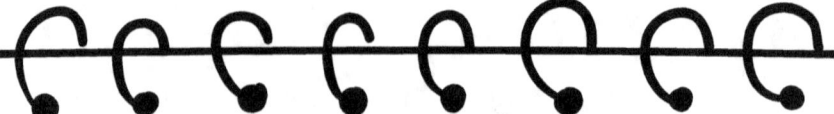

Service over Profit

"A business absolutely devoted to service will have only one worry about profits. They will be embarrassingly large."

HENRY FORD

EXPLANATION

Henry Ford, the founder of Ford Motor Company, revolutionized the automotive industry with his innovative approaches to production and business. His quote reflects the belief that prioritizing customer service and satisfaction will naturally lead to financial success. Ford's legacy is a testament to the idea that businesses thrive when they focus on meeting customer needs and delivering value. For entrepreneurs, this perspective encourages a service-first approach, where building strong relationships with customers can yield sustainable profitability and loyalty.

ACTION STEPS

Assess your customer service strategies and identify areas for improvement.

_____

_____

_____

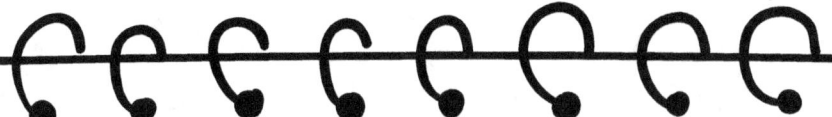

Taking Action

"Even if you are on the right track, you'll get run over if you just sit there."

WILL ROGERS

EXPLANATION

Will Rogers was a popular American cowboy, humorist, and actor known for his wit and insightful commentary on American life. His quote serves as a reminder that inaction can be detrimental, even when one is on a promising path. Rogers' humorous yet poignant observation emphasizes the need for continuous movement and effort in the face of opportunities and challenges. For entrepreneurs, this serves as a call to action, encouraging them to remain proactive and adaptable to navigate the dynamic landscape of business effectively.

ACTION STEPS

Identify one area of your business where you can take immediate action.

_____

_____

_____

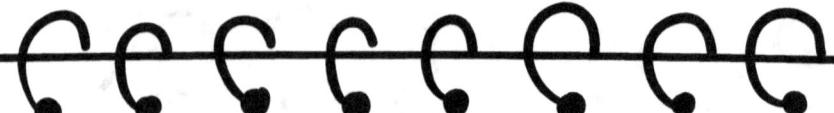

Think Big

"I like thinking big. If you're going to be thinking anything, you might as well think big."

DONALD TRUMP

EXPLANATION

Donald Trump, a businessman and former president of the United States, is known for his ambitious business ventures and larger-than-life persona. His quote encapsulates the idea that there is value in expansive thinking and bold aspirations. Trump's approach encourages individuals to set high goals and pursue them relentlessly. For entrepreneurs, thinking big can foster innovation and open new possibilities, pushing boundaries and challenging the status quo in their respective fields.

ACTION STEPS

Set a big goal for your business and outline the steps to achieve it.

_____

_____

_____

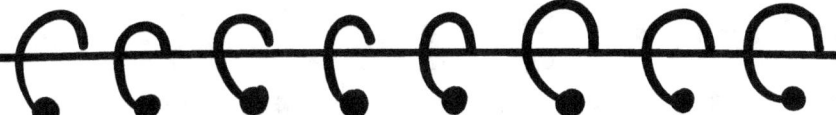

"The road to success and the road to failure are almost exactly the same."

COLIN R. DAVIS

EXPLANATION

Colin R. Davis was a prominent conductor and music educator who made significant contributions to the arts. His quote speaks to the fine line that often exists between success and failure, suggesting that the journeys are marked by similar challenges and decisions. This perspective reminds entrepreneurs that setbacks can be part of the process toward achieving their goals. Recognizing this reality can encourage resilience and a willingness to learn from failures, ultimately leading to greater successes.

ACTION STEPS

Reflect on a recent setback and identify lessons learned that can guide you.

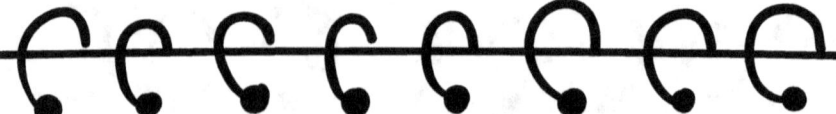

Meetings That Matter

"A meeting is an event at which the minutes are kept and the hours are lost."

UNKNOWN

EXPLANATION

This anonymous quote humorously critiques the often unproductive nature of meetings in the business world. It highlights the tendency for meetings to consume time without yielding significant results, a common frustration for many professionals. The sentiment resonates particularly with entrepreneurs who strive for efficiency and effectiveness in their operations. This quote encourages a reevaluation of how meetings are conducted, promoting a focus on actionable outcomes rather than mere discussions.

ACTION STEPS

Assess the necessity and structure of your upcoming meetings.

_____

_____

_____

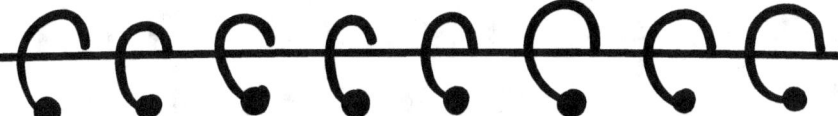

Thriving with Passion

"My mission in life is not merely to survive, but to thrive; and to do so with some passion, some compassion, some humor, and some style."

MAYA ANGELOU

EXPLANATION

Maya Angelou was an acclaimed poet, author, and civil rights activist whose powerful words and insights inspired generations. Her quote emphasizes the importance of living life fully and passionately, rather than just going through the motions. Angelou's philosophy encourages individuals to embrace their unique qualities and approach life with purpose. For entrepreneurs, this perspective serves as a reminder that success is not just about financial gain, but also about making a meaningful impact and enjoying the journey along the way.

ACTION STEPS

Reflect on what brings you joy and how you can incorporate more of it into your work.

_____

_____

_____

Impact of Emotional Connections

"I've learned that people will forget what you said, people will forget what you did, but people will never forget how you made them feel."

MAYA ANGELOU

EXPLANATION

Maya Angelou's profound insight into human connections emphasizes the importance of emotional impact in relationships. As a celebrated figure in literature and social justice, she understood that lasting impressions stem from genuine feelings and interactions. This quote holds particular significance in the business world, where customer relationships can dictate success. Entrepreneurs can harness this wisdom to create meaningful connections with clients and employees, focusing on empathy and understanding to foster loyalty and satisfaction.

ACTION STEPS

Consider how you can enhance emotional connections with your customers.

_____

_____

_____

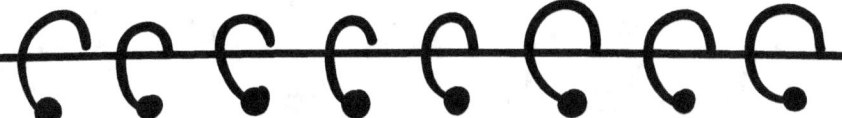

Start Where You Are

"Do what you can, with what you have, where you are."

THEODORE ROOSEVELT

EXPLANATION

Theodore Roosevelt, a dynamic leader and reformer, believed in the importance of action and resourcefulness. His quote encourages individuals to leverage their current circumstances and capabilities to effect change. Roosevelt's life exemplified the spirit of making the most of available resources, whether in politics or personal endeavors. For entrepreneurs, this serves as a powerful reminder that success is often built on utilizing existing strengths and opportunities, rather than waiting for perfect conditions.

ACTION STEPS

Identify a small action you can take today with your current resources.

_____

_____

_____

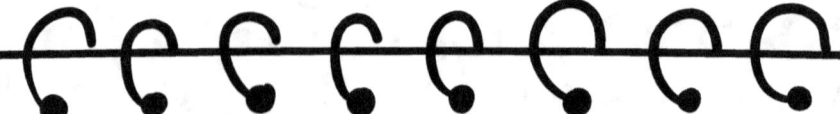

Focus on Inner Strength

"What lies behind us and what lies before us are tiny matters compared to what lies within us."

RALPH WALDO EMERSON

EXPLANATION

Ralph Waldo Emerson was a 19th-century American essayist and philosopher who emphasized the significance of individualism and inner strength. His quote speaks to the importance of self-awareness and the power of personal attributes in navigating life's challenges. Emerson's philosophy encourages individuals to focus on their inner resources rather than external circumstances. For entrepreneurs, this insight reinforces the idea that confidence, resilience, and a strong sense of self can significantly impact their ability to succeed and adapt in the business world.

ACTION STEPS

Reflect on your inner strengths and how they have contributed to your success.

_____

_____

_____

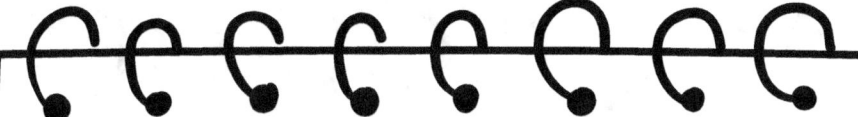

Key to Success

"Action is the foundational key to all success."

PABLO PICASSO

EXPLANATION

Pablo Picasso, one of the most influential artists of the 20th century, revolutionized the art world with his innovative approaches. His quote underscores the importance of taking decisive action as the cornerstone of achieving success. Picasso's prolific career exemplifies how continuous effort and experimentation can lead to groundbreaking outcomes. For entrepreneurs, this serves as a call to prioritize action over mere planning, reinforcing the idea that success is driven by taking initiative and moving forward, even amidst uncertainty.

ACTION STEPS

Identify a specific action you can take toward your biggest goal today.

_____

_____

_____

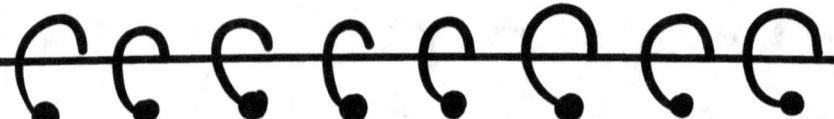

Perseverance through Challenges

"If you are going through hell, keep going."

WINSTON CHURCHILL

EXPLANATION

Winston Churchill, the British Prime Minister during World War II, is celebrated for his leadership and oratory skills in times of crisis. His quote reflects the importance of resilience and perseverance, especially in challenging situations. Churchill's steadfastness inspired a nation during its darkest hours, emphasizing the need to push through difficulties rather than succumb to despair. For entrepreneurs, this perspective encourages a tenacity that can turn setbacks into stepping stones, reinforcing the value of endurance in the face of adversity.

ACTION STEPS

Think of a current challenge and list three ways to keep moving forward.

_____

_____

_____

NOTE

NOTE

NOTE

NOTE

NOTE

Thank You For Your Order